MEANDERING MEADOWS

THE JOY OF POETRY

LALITA VAITHEESWARAN

Made with ♥ on the Notion Press Platform
www.notionpress.com

Contents

Contents

Contents

Contents

Acknowledgements

I stand in gratitude towards my family for all the support that I got for this and all my endeavors.

I thank my friends who have been my encouragement in all my ventures.

I am thankful to the Almighty for keeping me under divine benevolence.

My thanks to ***Notion Press*** for its support in publishing this book.

My gratitude to *Unsplash.com* for all the pictures used in this book.

1. Gratitude

I have been showered with benevolence galore
I bow to the Supreme and cannot ask for more
Grateful to the universe for every morsel
For the scattering happiness by family cheerful
For the naughty friends whom I treasure
Their love in their wit that can't be measured
For the sunny mornings those wake me up in the pink
Dexterity coupled with good ideas to think
For the lesser privileged who help me ever
The sundry and errands on time to deliver
For every one spreading joy and cheer
Making my life happy worth being here.
I know not how to reciprocate my gratitude
As my heart is overwhelmed with feelings plentitude
Trying to gather them in multitude

2. A stranger who came to my town

Uncanny looks, demeanor eerie and disheveled hair,
He came on a dark winter night from nowhere
Stealthily as a shadowy silhouette he crept in credence
Drenched in conceit, his vanity overflowing in abundance
He sneered at all, and looked down upon his peer
Materialistic belongings were his flaunting flair
His thunderous laughter that was sarcastic and snide
Made everyone pull their tatters on their bare to hide
I enquired him where was his gesture humane?
Why does he lug himself with vices and bane?
He roared with a laughter evil, that resounded and echoed
He suddenly then pulled out a mirror and showed
Shockingly I saw it was me, a facsimile of him identical
Appallingly, I had changed into my doppelganger evil
How bitterly I had become a stranger in my own eyes
Worsening from a human to a beast, living a world of lies

3. Colours

Hues of different tinges, red blue and green
Splashed across the air making the azure kaleidoscopic
The aura is splendid, there is a twinge of excitement
Blue skies above and red earth below
Spraying on every parched soul, thirsty today
Good will and positive vibes embrace each other with warmth
It's the festival of colors they say
The triumph of goodness over badness is in sway
The colours are of love, of affection that bonds
Every religion and people reaffirm their fondness
Colours in water spill to drench
Washing away hostility till hearts are cleansed
Colours are not mere colours, they are symbols of love
They paint the earth down and the heavens above

4. Daughters

Precious progeny, priceless posterity
O daughters! you are the mantle of days to come
You give birth to a whole new generation
The foundation of a civilization you build to blossom
Frolicking and playing in the parents' home
Pampered and loved by one and all
You spread cheer, love and happiness around
Without you the home lacks a soul
You become the spreader of joy when you marry
Your other home now becomes your own
You handle responsibilities entirely new to you
Emotionally supported or sometimes alone
And yet you aren't welcome at birth by your own
Your biological vulnerability is misused by many
You are groped, molested, raped abused and burned
Blamed for every incident unsavory or uncanny
Daughters! You need to stand up for yourself
Refusing to take injustice lying down ever
Remember silence would never lead you anywhere
Fight for justice and speak up against the perpetrator

5. The last meeting

With invasive tubes and gadgets those beeped
Only on paper he was alive
The progressive painful disease was taking its toll
On medicines and fluids did he thrive
The doctors, all, with faces grim
Examined him with a thud and a pinch
There was an eager wait for a miraculous response
Waiting to see him wince and flinch
The attorney, and the kith and kin
Gathered round him near the hospital bed
Waiting for him to sign his will
Who knows when he'd be pronounced dead
When darkness fell and silence reigned
All but the wife left him alone for the night
He grimaced and moved his hand to signal
That he wanted to set things straight and right
The attorney was let in as doctors rushed
He signed a paper in his meeting last
He had bequeathed his all to an orphanage,his home
As everyone else looked aghast

6. The day for love

Let love be always in the air
Why make it a one-day affair?
Love not only others but yourself too
Pamper yourself and give yourself a facelift new
Let love from within you emanate
Go with your ownself on a beautiful date
Get some chocolates if you so desire
Spend your own money to set passions afire
Roses you buy a bunch not one
Let the rose seller too bask under the sun
Go to the old age homes where yesteryears dwell
Listen with patience to the stories they tell
Visit the orphanages to give them a hug
Listen to your heart strings giving a tug
Love every one around, joys afar you spray
Give it any name, but let it be each n every day

7. The song of my heart

Chords of harmony and musical symphony
Rhythmic waves of unparalleled, exalted, ecstasy
Lyrical refrains reverberated in resonance
As melodious chimes played in assonance
I whistled in glee as I watched the vast horizon
The sun was playing hide and seek with balls of cotton
The swish and swoosh of the breeze made trees dance
The silhouettes in sunshine were dazed in a trance
Chirpy birds and butterflies sang the tune of gaiety
A rustle of dried leaves went jubilant in tranquility
The golden ball was turning orange as it set
An eventide in twilight in paradise they met
The blue sky held twinkling stars in rhapsody and bliss
As the milky white celestial moon twirled to kiss
I'm singing to the tune of nature mystical magical
Liberated like a minstrel, a gypsy soul ethereal.

8. Spring sprite

Her ethereal elixir of life brings out
The essence of ambrosial ecstasy
Frosted and lifeless beings are now
Singing the song of life anew
Blooms and blossoms fragrance in the air perfuse
Breezy winds whistling past, whisper sweet nothings
Leaves are in a trance as they jubilate in joy
Spring gives them a new breath of life
Like a potion miraculous and magical
Nature dances in celebration and joyful glee
The spring sprite is the fairy elf who loves
Colorful hues of green and red, painting the earth
Her creation is limitless as she renews life
Hugging every creature on earth she rejoices
Basking in the sprightly sunshine of spring.

9. The photo album

Lost time like footprints on sand
Peeped through the sepia pictures
The childhood and the youth mocked
At my wrinkled and furrowed crow's feet
An era of life which I lived just for others
My smiles, my laughter and my happiness weren't mine
Expended and exhausted prime time to nurture
Converting a scattered haven of disarray into a home
Chirpy chimes and hearty peals of laughter resounded
Reverberating and disappearing into bizarre lands beyond the horizon
Bringing back to life those lively moments of joy
When every corner of the abode was cozy with warmth
Where is it now? Lost in no-man's land of uncertainty
As I rocked on my easy chair with misty eyes
The photo album hazed merging into oblivion of my memories

10. Festival of colors

Splashed with colors red green and blue
Spraying gulal and colors completely drenching you
Dholak and phaag vibrating in the air
Everyone adult or children a warm camaraderie share
Sweets and snacks special add to the zeal
Sweetness mixed with taste, a gastronomic appeal
A laughing spree stems or is it the bhang?
Intoxicated with joy of spring is the crazy gang
Holi, the festival of colors smeared with tender care
Every religion, caste and creed a brotherhood share
Every bad feeling or enmity of the past
Holi promises that these would never last
It's a time to embrace and hug with fondness dear
Holi we wait for you with excitement every year

11. The village road

Narrow lanes and dusty roads twirling undauntedly
Welcoming the chiming clangs of bullock carts which ply
Kissing the skirting tall eucalyptus trees along
A living testimony to every passer by
Climbing up and down tortuous terrains,
Wild cacti and prickly flowers that caress with warmth
Carefully attaining the destination in its zig-zag
A gust of dust that leaves a trail of the path
Cow dung cakes and huts daubed in mud
The village roads know every inside story
As they twist and turn in hairpin bends
They groan with pain to every atrocity gory
Many children, the roads in their laps carried
To escort them to the urban pastures green
Leaving behind ebbing ponds and drying wells
Attracted to the glimmering silvery sheen
Now deserted, the roads await and hope
A reverse brain-drain back to the village someday
They keep their spirits alive with fallen flowers
Some distant footsteps, and some strands of hay!

12. Love is in the air

The cuckoo is shaking its head in glee
It is singing a song about you and me
The breeze whistles as it tugs my trembling core
It nestles me into an embrace as warm as yours
I am laughing as I tread on the pastures green
The petrichor and the silver drops keeping its sheen
The birds glide with a whisper as they soar high
Their ecstatic chatter and chirp echo from the sky
The Pansies and the Tulips are wavering in delight
Rejoicing in happy moments appears everything in sight
Milky white moon bathed in shiny silver hue
The creation seems to be talking about me and you
I feel blissful, idyllic as I my soul bare
I feel your presence, your love is in the air!

13. Acrostic-Valentine

Vibrant verses of love exchanged
Ardently ornate with jewels of warmth
Longings of hearts that pulsate in joy
Ecstatic embraces that yearn for more
New promises that bond lovers anew
Threads delicate that need nurturing
Invigorating and intense passions flow
Navigating through waters not always calm
Effervescent happiness that lives forever.

14. Sins of the patriarch

Bursting with egoistic pride, vanity clouding his psyche
He sought no girlchild in the womb of his wife
Ordering for her slaughter before she could breathe
The womb turned tomb for the unborn fetus
She'd metamorphose into a beautiful damsel for him in the night
Yet he was unsatiated of the lust he bore,
Going in search of his unfulfilled desires which oft raised their heads
Visiting brothels, whorehouses and those of ill repute
Reveling and basking in the desires of his lecherous demeanor while
The inquisitive neighbor watched, sympathizing with the unfortunate wife
Visiting her to stand in solidarity with her in dawns and dusks of her heyday
The compassion soon turned into an evil passion emblazing two souls
Her parched essence discovered an oasis of love in him and they merged
'Twas her moment of liberation and his' a jubilation of winning over another woman
The infuriated husband fumed and fretted as his manly pride was hurt,
Couldn't see a wife's smiles and happiness without his presence
A grisly shadow of violence and anger ensued between them,
Fury and rage reigned in the kingdom and abode
Miseries to abate and glorify the infidel, the lover connived
Dripping in gory sanguine blood, killing her conscience, his mortal body lay

Standing testimony to the cardinal sins, committed in the roots of patriarchy

Published in international magazine FASIHI

https://www.fasihimag.com/post/the-sins-of-the-patriarch-a-poem-by-laita-vaitheeswaram

15. The beautiful cosmos

Colours of the rainbow splash across skies
A spectrum of divine charming hues rise

The orange ball is peeping from above
slowly setting to bid adieu with love

Tricky twilight smiles ready to disguise
A crimson azure soothing to the eyes

Darkness is in queue asking dusk to shove
Starry heavens will witness the moon rove

16. The color of love

Reds, magentas, rainbow hue, love sparkles like ornate dew
Passionate and pure with innocence galore, feelings are mutually true
The golden shimmers and shine, depicting the highest love divine
Noble souls rising in prayers, goodwill silently percolating the airs
Parents and child bond, with tinges and colours well beyond
Unconditional love packed in pink, overflowing up-to the brink
Preened pruned and bloomed, as emotions of blissful joy loomed
Brotherhood, goodwill and camaraderie, every color is sprinkled free
Then comes in the sinister grey, throwing every virtue at bay
Love becomes the jealousy green, possessiveness adding to its sheen
Blind love can see colors none, only after a whim it does run
Suddenly it turns red; avarice and hatred killing it dead
Oh love! why don't you remain, crystal pure and sane?
Let love be only white, without evil intent in sight.

17. The light of knowledge

She peeped through the pane, in wonder and awe
All eyes were glued to books
knowledge being imparted, was all she saw
Hope shone through bright new looks
Young teaching the old, as she dropped her jaw
household helps, drivers, cooks
To stay afloat this was, her but last straw
No more hiding in nooks
Education empowered women
she realized now
A brighter sketch of future, she could draw
Clear vault and flowing brooks
The sky's the limit
Freedom from the claw
of cozeners and crooks

18. Acrostic-Dauntless

Dare devils determined to stay their grounds
Able leaders, who show others the way
Unstoppable are they once they are resolved
Never say die is their motto for life
Tirelessly working towards their goals
Large-hearted who live for goodness and virtue
Errant perpetrators are brought to the fore
Standing fearless against all odds for justice
Sacrifices for a good cause they dont hesitate to make

19. Celestial rapture

The evening delved into a misty tryst
An orange glow stemmed from the setting sun
Leaves and flowers swayed in a trance
basking in the crepuscular glow of twilight
The azure vault looked ethereal and sublime
As the starry sky threw an angelic look
The gibbous smiled as it hid behind the cloak
Bidding the tired eventide a cheery farewell
The fragrant breeze spread aromatic whiffs
Tugging at every heart string in ecstasy
Harmonious rhapsody, the soul crooned
My pneuma and nature were in symphony
The mystique of the creations divine
enrapturing the spirit in ebullient joy
Silhouettes and shadows of merry hearts
Entwined in seraphic, celestial embraces

20. Season of love

There is an aura of happiness everywhere
Fragrance of roses percolating the air
It's a season of love, a season divine
A time to show one's love to the valentine
Cozy cuddles of sweethearts and their blushing cheeks
A day of saying "Yes I do" to those love who seek
Yearning hearts will be together to pine
Hey will you be my beloved Valentine?
Sweet nothings whispered and promises made
Building memories of happiness that would never fade
Indulgence in luxurious gifts and intoxicating wine
Hand in hand go the celebrating Valentines
My Valentine, I search you in the thickets of my dreams
This day, every year, is an eon it seems
You are an elusive illusion, you're my sunshine
Oh my dear Valentine will you be mine?

21. The journey called life

Life is a journey full of variegated display
Tumultuous roads and tranquility together in array
The supreme bestows upon us, both darkness and light
It's upon us to endow the sparkles -cheerful and bright
Imbue and imbibe the fragrance of the sunshine every day.
Thorns and petals both lie scattered on your way
Ecstatic moments splattered amid moments of dismay
If there's a luminous day there's going to be a night
Life is a journey!
When from you, the golden sunlight gradually drifts away
The evening of life, with its frightful claws, remains with you to stay
Those wandering, fleeting moments which made memoirs of delight
Open your soul to the realities of enlightening insight
Accepting the truth of life, let all fears allay
Life is a journey!

22. Acrostic-Deception

Dark shadows reigned over the orbit
Eerie silence added to the woes
Camouflaging what was real and true
Evasive manoeuvres which were distorted
Paving a way leading into gloomy obscurity
Treachery which couldn't be gauged
Illusions which promised an alluring world
Ornate and glittery full of deceit
Nothing that met the eyes was real!

23. The mystical marvel

The blue kite soared high
and reached the rainbow skies
As the child tugged it
to ascend to the crest
The stubborn thread swayed
amid ecstatic cries
The excited kid jumped
in jubilant zest
Go kite go! and kiss
the fragrant balmy breeze
touching the zenith
and gauging mighty seas
Come back to tell me
celestial azure tales
Arcane allegories
hidden under veils.

24. My night terror

Desolate empty streets which looked uncanny
While I wandered through them deserted, alone
unknown, queer faces greeted me with odd eyes
'Twas a total world of Strangers which was forlorn
Purple clouds began hovering starlit skies
My locale, my memory failed to fathom
My heart raced; adrenaline began to rise
Dread, dismay, panic gripped my entire system
Heavens! I prayed reciting prayers many
Startled, petrified that amnesia had seized
Woke to the nightmare of ***Alzheimer's disease.***

25. The joy of living

Vessel full to the brim
feared of overflowing
lest there is a deluge
flooding of feelings huge
wreaking havoc evil
unsuspectedly spills!

Of your emotions
wounding as vile oceans
shredding virtuous souls
creating painful goals
scarred anima remains
Reverberating pains!

Joyful liberations
cheerful jubilations
live and let each one live
just bountiful love give
Let's celebrate this life
without hatred or strife!

26. God is near

Unanswered questions which knot as mysteries
Peculiar and eerie as they might surreptitiously appear
An aura of uncertainties that dwell in hearts of many
Ominous yet being unraveled on its own isn't that queer?
Dark valleys and abysses with daunting paths
Shaking the core of the soul out of fear
A stretch of time that heals the scars of the scary past
Replacing melancholy and sadness in to a blissful cheer
Rainbow skies after a holocaust that emptied vast terrains
Bouncing back and striving to wipe away every tear
The miracles that are seen in everyday life
Remind us of the supreme and infinite powers here
Every little whisper, every little drop of dew
A prayer on the lips and goodness in hearts for dears
Whatever will be will be, and you cannot change it
It's our faith in the bountiful, that God is near!

27. Acrostic-Humanity

Hallowed intentions and deeds
Unique in its demeanour
Magnanimous is the heart
Ability to embrace without bias
Noble to its core
Ideal to emulate by all
Teaching how to make the world affable
Yardstick of Utopia

28. The super woman

It's high time we let go the labels and tags
That we give to the women to hold her in esteem
Let her be a simpleton, a human who also has feelings
She may be vulnerable and not strong as she seems
She is no super woman who multitasks with ease
And juggles every chore with nimble alacrity
She can slipup too or forget and create a blunder
For the mistake committed, holding no guilt or pity
She is no Goddess or symbol of purity beyond compare
She can also be tempted, tested or beguiled as anyone
Falling a prey to the traps and snares laid
For erring beyond absolution, do not from deference shun
She can also be hungry and tired at the end of the day
As she carries the load of her endless sweat
She may want to be the first to eat before the man or child
She needs equity more than equality, not anyone's fume or fret
No! she does not want to compete or surpass any man to win
She asks only what to her in these years was due
She just wants her own space, some freedom and her say
The woman is a human just like me and you !!

29. Fountain of youth

Wrinkled face and aged demeanor, forehead full of creases
Trembling gait, uncertainty looming, as every frolic ceases
Fear and melancholy, grip the hearts, as youth starts to fly
Alas! there could be an ambrosia that could age defy
The old man walked up to the fountain that oozes out youth
He was cautioned that he'd be young but just for a moment or two
Anxious and curious to get back the vigor and the zeal
He drank from the fountain just to see how he feels
Hey presto! he changed to a young charming bloke
Was this a miracle? Or was it just a lucky stroke?
He was dripping from juvenile sap, as his alacrity rose
Brimming with unabated joy for the marvel he chose
Swiftly, crumpled furrows and lines made home as before
In the blink of an eye, the lively attractive young man was no more
Youth is just a fleeting, momentary, gateway to the old n uncouth
Every stage of life is precious -there's no fountain of youth!

30. Wit or wisdom?

Today's life stares at uncertainties and disenchantment
There's strife, sadness and melancholy everywhere
Tempers run high with vanishing empathies for fellowmen
Neighbors live like strangers who for each other do not care
The spectrum tips towards dwindling mental well-being
No goodness or laughter to keep people in good cheer
Worries of the future, doubts about life's unpredictability
Heralding towards doom, every move of life would steer
Then in walked wit, with its share of pun and fun
Engaging folks with splits of hilarious amusement and delight
The fragrant breeze was laden with blissful ecstasy
The moroseness and gloominess were cut by divine sprite
Wisdom and wit walk hand in hand, no one's better
Both are needed to complement each other here
The experiences nurtured in the bosom of the yore
Needs to be quick-witted to spread goodwill and cheer

31. The power of miracles

The magic of miracles brings in wonder
That which no one ever could have marveled
Appearing as a gust of fresh breeze
Changing one's perspective and outlook towards life.
Miracles are felt in day to day lives
It may not be a gigantic turnaround
The small and trivial changes of destiny
Can be experienced as something which saved lives.
Why one was saved in an earthquake?
Or why is one alive even after that dreaded illness?
Why did our life not turn turtle and shun us?
Why in that split second , we crossed that bridge which later collapsed
Miracles are our will power, our faith in the Supreme
Miracles are our paths taken to carve a better destiny
Miracles are saviors that help us look with gratitude
Miracles give us the impetus to live on , when the world closes doors
The power of miracles is immense as it is connected to hope
Hope that lets us smile even in the darkest night
Let's not give up, let us believe in miracles and its power
Every moment of life hinges on miracles as it changes into hour

32. Do not light it up blue

As she lay on the couch with dread and fear
She had in her womb a pulsating heart dear
Clinging to her soul with a cord thin
She was nurturing her with her own life from within
Some tests, some scans, some medicines said they
Would reveal whether your offspring is here to stay
Her tears incessant, she held on to her bosom tight
No! it's her life, her blood, her living might
My baby shall live and it's my right to say
No one can take my heartbeats away
She ran and fled to hide under the thicket nest
Until she had her baby to her chest
The baby when she cried, had the momma in pain
The smiles of the young one had bliss running in veins
The joys were short-lived as it was declared
The baby is autistic while her bleeding soul bared
The home and the crib has to be lit up blue today
As the whole world would wake up into awareness this day
The mother sobbed and cried while she pleaded to all
Blue, red or pink , or any color is my call
My baby's no puzzle that you're going to solve and crack
It's plain empathy and sensitivity that you lack
Inclusiveness and care is all what she wants
Your *Lighting up Blue* is what scaringly daunts

The "Light It Up Blue" (LIUB) initiative is intended to raise international awareness of autism in support of Autism Awareness Month in the United States.

33. Introspection

Delving deep into my self, I found a dark abyss in conceal
Shadowy crevices of pain, scars those refused to heal
Warm lotions and balmy creams found no base to stay
The more my wounds were soothed, the more they gave way
The light from the celestia reverted back to the skies
The valley within, not letting it pass through the pretense and lies
Darkness and melancholy were all that which shrouded the anima
There was scarcity of happiness as despair clung to my pneuma
The subdued voice of conscience was lying in dismay
As there was no room for positivity or a shining ray
I kept silent as I contemplated and closed my eyes in thought
Realized that joys need freedom and not shackles of narrow-minded knots
That negativity and pessimism are uninvited floating guests
They find root when we allow them to rest
Our mind is a garden with blossom and bloom
Let it nurture only happiness and see ecstatic bliss flow
It is we who let gloominess set in and let happiness go.

34. My doppelganger

She looked back and stared at me
Partly in anger, partly in concern
No, there's no need to masquerade and hide
It's high time you learn to discern
Why that broad smile of pretense?
When you are reeling under pain
It's not strength what you're showing the world
The wounds show on surface again

I looked back at her and was aghast
Grey hair and wrinkles had taken a toll
Is that the real me? it was unbelievable
Sunken eyes and a bleeding, dripping soul
I blinked to see if things were real
Those teary eyes blinked on me too
Both of us needed a catharsis in this life
As we hugged our alter-egos true.

35. Questions

Softly and subtly, it asks questions
On everything you do
Showing you the mirror of your soul
Whether you are blatantly true
It pauses your every step you take
Making you on your wrongs and rights ponder
If you listen and heed to its incessant nags
You were just going to slip, you wonder
Questions asked are to keep you virtuous
The say that echoes and reverberates from within
The inner voice-our conscience inside us
Has its opinion resonated even in a din
Pause and answer every question it asks
You are then bound not to lose your way
It's stringent morality, it's ethical outlook
Shall never let one ever go astray

36. The world outside my window

Trapped in the rigmarole of the daily grind
I had no time to happiness and joys find
Stuck in the narrow labyrinthine maze
All the emotions were misplaced in haze
Fatigued and tired as I looked out to take a whiff
Ahh! the lavender, the fragrant breeze and petrichor I could sniff
I was lost in the buzz of the bees and butterflies
As they dived to suck nectar from wild flowers from skies
They exuded gay abandon as they swirled across to and fro
The paths of green weeds, inflorescence and flowerets and more
Iridescent blooms that swayed in the soft breeze
Was humming a melody for the ears to please
I watched in amazement, as I sat in solitude
My head bowed to the bountiful nature in gratitude

37. Letter to papa

Papa when will you come back to take us back home?
Hiding from the enemies, we're tired as we aimlessly roam
Momma said she was having a small baby inside her
Hunger and thirst dominating, this war cannot but deter
Papa, I have dropped out of school as they need recruits new
I held the rifle heavy and was just one among the few
My feet feel sore after I was made to run an extra mile
We were threatened and abused, much to our rile
Whose fault it is papa? Are we not her sons?
Why were we invaded and why were you, with them, made to run?
Papa, the home looks void with a few bullet holes on walls
One more bombarding in the sky and it is sure to fall
I saw a heap of rubble under which little Ashley lay
He had come a wandering to look at the skies, people here say
Every siren, every bugle sends a chill down our spines, shaken
Every night as we lie down on floor, we are not sure to awaken
Why can't we live in peace? Why do we need a war?
It has wounded, it has scathed, leaving a gaping scar.

38. Noisy words

Words are messages which have magic
They're destined to bring fervor and zeal
Some become loud to bring on enthusiasm
While others are soft and subtle to heal
Some are understandable with gestures
And need not come out of their lair
Their mere existence and presence spell the outcome
And they are laden with empathetic care
Words that are redundant or insinuate
Racism, sarcasm, sexism or hate
Need not be unzipped from the closed arena
Lest they should unleash a loathing spate
Words should hit the nail on the head
So that only the essence is conveyed as a whole
Love begets love and so does hatred
Let's not injure a bleeding soul
Love is difficult a virtue to win
Let words not lose its charm of tact
The use of words or the lack of it
Is the one that makes or breaks a pact

39. Scars which bleed

The wounds were raw, she was writhing in pain
She walked up to everyone, to cry and complain
They looked on and rolled their eyes in dismay
Where are the wounds? Show us we pray!
Her tears overflowed as she was trying to heal
Her fresh gaping wounds she was trying to conceal
They looked indifferent and questioned her intent
They found pretense and flamboyance in her content
Why can't we see all that you're trying to show?
How is it that we cannot comprehend or know?
Look at us, we are complete in flesh and skin
There is enormous strength outside and massive one within
No ! she cried as she in the open bared her soul
My wounds are scars are not seen as they've wounded my whole
My scars are seen by those of you who empathize with me
Every tear that drops from the eyes, is my soul's elegy

40. The guiding light

There is always light at the end of darkness
There may be patches of strife
Woes and worries that create havoc
Tumbled heavens and catastrophic waves
That settles down in time to come
There is always light that shows the way
In darkness where the minds are numb
The choices from the right and the wrong
Is like a overwhelming quagmire of sorts
The weak shimmer turns brighter and clear
There is always light which guides the misled
It's the psyche that refuses to admit
When there is redundance of evil and wicked feelings
The pride and the ego as they take the lead
Turning a blind eye to all that's bright
The light always brightens its surroundings
Removing any shadow of ignorance
Open minds, uncluttered thoughts accept the truth
Following the burning candle as it sways its candescence
To integrate all that is dark and murky

41. The conjurer

The sweltering sun with its raging heat
Was in no vein to take defeat
Swiftly the white balls of clouds wandered
Changing their hue, they turned gray and meandered
A slight drizzle changed into a pour
Suddenly the winds gushed into a roar
A small Robin with a twig in its beak
Hopped hither and thither on the creek
Glossy plumaged birds chirped with joyous melody
Behind clumpsof ferns and thickets creating rhapsody
Faint, far-off sounds of the whistling breeze looked enchanting
The Ivy cottage with its majestic façade was entrancing
Nature turned a sorcerer, conjuring an ethereal spree
'Look mommy rains have created magic', shouted my child in glee

42. The truth

Truth and lies were walking hand in hand
Truth was naked while lies was covered in layers
Both as they ambled through thickets and streams
Truth felt the prick as it was bare
Fragrant ribbons and ornate attire lies wore
As she bowed in front of a wooing crowd
Truth was despised and kept aloof
As lies enjoyed her glossy gossamer shroud
Everyone cheered and happily screamed
Lies was showing them the garden of Eden
Truth tried to heckle and disrupt the cozy show
But people never wanted to see what was hidden
Truth opened its mouth to utter reality
It was getting suffocated without a gush
Lies stared and arm twisted her partner
And coerced truth to remain hush-hush
Truth knows no bounds and does not stay dormant
It shouted to the people and mirror show
People went giddy headed as many collapsed
As there was a melee and a huge row
The old realized how they're being ill treated
The child her biological parents discovered
The wife found out about her husband's infidel ways
The husband shocked how only his money was revered
Mayhem and pandemonium ruled the land

As lies choked to death on the floor
Truth did not know whether all this was worth
How much truth was lesser or more.

43. Color me green

The green of nature and of growth
Enchants me as I sit in the dark ravine
Groping to envisage the colorful dreams
Pulling me towards it
The greens of fertility and life
Teach me how life is a never-ending circle
And how nothing is lost but only created
The green of renewal and resurrection
Tells me there is still hope
Nothing has been lost but can be mended
And the beautiful creation subsists
The one green that is my bane
Is the one of jealousy insane
Sowing seeds of hatred and separation
Colours everything in shades of gray
Color me green so that life is vibrant
And in everyone, love I see.

44. Your eyes and me

Those iridescent ravishing beautiful eyes
In which I could see an image of me
Like a valley of fragrant lavender that edged
An oasis which soothed my mind
Their irresistible search everywhere and beyond
The little wet ocean that twinkled
To tell me your unfathomable love
The heavenly dazzle which fascinated
And dragged me into the magnetic well
I could live there forever, feeling your endearing togetherness
If only eyes could speak, there were volumes of words
To tell how much they were in pursuit
To keep me and my love floating in those enchanting ravines
As I hold on to those mesmerizing latches,
You shut your eyes and imprison me forever
Now you and me together see the world
Your eyes and my reflection in them

45. Life

The vagaries of life, intrigue every soul curious
Why, what and how does it portray its purpose?
Sometimes it is smooth-sailing with happy vibes
At other times there is misery, sadness and strife
Arduous paths sometimes put us to tests
Breaking the morale even before concluding our quest
The ups and downs of life make us a person improved well
Teaching us patience, fortitude and endurance to dwell
Life is like an examination teaching us to challenges face
To bounce back and walk on even after a fall from grace
Life is a song to sing in gay abandon carefree
The melody set to tune with inner peace and harmony
Laughter can the tough hindrances of life tackle
The deterrents and difficulties are erased like miracles
Life is sometimes a deal without an answer strange
The mindset towards life can make the view change
Sometimes life does not give you all that you ask
You chase it only to realize that it's an unattainable task
Our dreams we live as we move on in life each day
Life is a challenge, as everyone negotiates one's way
Let us all see life as just a joyous ride
Living it with zeal and taking it in our stride

46. No more tears

Salty water that rises and ebbs from eyes
Tumultuous emotions creating turbulence till it dries
When the pain is immense and intolerable
There are flashes when the dams are let open
Drowning every emotion, every cry of despair
There is no one to share the letdown, no one to care
Oh, tears you dare not spill out of my eyes
The memories of the yore would make me hollow again
Leave me in the lurch crying in pain
Those nightmares that I want to get rid of
Lie on the surface, ready to deluge and pour
Those shattered dreams and those moments of brutality
Which lie sealed under my eyelids briefly
Which are triggered with every memory that passes
No more tears now and no more delving into the past
No more churning of turmoil and bleeding of the esse
No more ......Not any more

47. Festival of new beginnings -Vishu

A time for joy and to rejoice as spring arrives
A time of equinox and beauty to view
A time for the farmers to harvest their fields
The festival marks a beginning new
The festival marks decorating the altar
With cereals, fruits and vegetables green
Gold and silver and an idol of Krishna with '***Konna poo***'(Laburnum)
A mirror that enhances the sheen
This is readied a night before, before retiring to bed
No one's allowed to see anything else before
As you come and stand in the front of the lighting lamp
You open your eyes and see the beautiful '***Kani***" kept on the floor
Then the elders of the house bless you with '***Kayineetam***"
A gift of gold or money as may be
Festivities and an elaborate feast then follows
With '***Payasam', 'pappadam' and 'maanga curry***'
Vishu signifies prosperity and abundance
Every household wishes that they live cheerfully
May Lord Krishna bless each and every soul
The beginning shall lead the whole year into glee.

48. The pinnacle of love

I tried to love you less, I couldn't
Your irrepressible charm and your enchanting smile
Triggered in me emotions insuppressible
As your oasis of love encircled my life's isle
Love was in abundance as it flooded
From heart to heart as overflowing urns
It was gushing and springing and cascading to pour
Connecting yearning souls as intimacy it churned
Bountiful and generous, aplenty galore
My love can never be enough for a lifetime
As I pine for you and nurse a yearning heart
I too can feel your enchanting love sublime
Unfathomable, unmeasurable, can it ever reach a zenith?
Can the trickle, dribble and drizzle, overflow and spill?
When an inexhaustible, limitless cornucopia of fondness
Is growing into a never ending, limitless, unfailing fill?
I tried to love you less, I couldn't
I'd be a void if my heart goes into desolate terrains
Babbles and gurgles of emotional spouts
Are sprinkling on their own to drench you in rain
My heart dreams and loves you ceaselessly
I have no hold on my eternally pouring core
My love for you shall never reach a pinnacle
It will only grow into more and more.

49. The mother earth

Bounties of blessings and fathomless benedictions
She gives every one for the whole life
Unconditional like our mothers, she expects nothing in return
Only that we do not destroy her ever
For mother earth has other children to look after
Flora and fauna and the innumerable creatures small
But we ,human beings, in our self-centered goals
Wanted to make this earth a concrete jungle
Mother earth begged and pleaded fervently
But humans were lost in their greed and pride
Tall buildings and dams, forests were cut,
as we wanted more and more
We destroyed her, snatched her essence
Forgetting that the more we corner her
We are going to be the sufferers forever
Today we yearn for greens and leaves
For flowing rivers which are full
For weather that is cooler
With no unpredictable disasters
Let us pledge to save mother earth!

50. Different strokes

1

Semblance of love, coated in pretense
The fervor of love when lost its essence
She was going through pain and torture every day
Tying her soul in captivity and fray
When the heart does not beat the rhythms perish
When the soul is scarred, there's nothing to cherish
Clinging on to a thin hope of renewed tomorrow
She was only betrayed and surrounded by sorrow

2

Her heart still beat for her sweetheart in the hills
Where their dreams and aspirations had overflown to spill
Their different cultures had then been the bone of contention
Snatched from each other's hands there was separation
She wanted to live and not die each day breaking down
Gathering her courage and her wedding gown,
She ran to meet her beau on the lake near the hills
Where he had called her to rekindle the old thrill
The night was passionate full of cravings and desire
There was passionate embraces and zealous fire
Souls were in union as love spread in the air
Everything in war or love is fair!

51. Hope

I stood there shattered in the hope of a new dawn
Tears incessant, recurring pain of a forlorn
The world looked like a murky abyss to me
Dark shadows of gloom clinging my essence empty
Black clouds loomed above threatening to pour
My scarred soul shouted- not anymore
I saw a figure like my own standing before me
Who stood like a tough figurine of bravery
It wiped my tears and gave me strength immense
Gather courage of your own and don't live in pretense
Stand up, and face your perpetrators in their eyes
Break your silence and expose them and their lies
This was my alter-ego who had come to my spirit raise
Today I am proud that everyone I've the courage to face

52. Stay away

Those days when I struggled to pay me fees
Buying a new book was a far-fetched dream sour
I went to the downtown market to get hold
of abandoned books not needed by students anymore
My shoes tattered, worn-out, resounded
With stories of penury that I endured in life
Step by step, ladder by ladder I was carefully climbing
Weary with destitution, hunger and strife
I remember the sharp pain of humiliation
That day, when I knocked at your door
You slammed the gate on my face and disappeared
Even as failing to recognize your friend of yore
I remember those days of utter disgrace
When every kin to recognize me declined
As I staggered with a torn slipper and a shirt
As I turned my back, you heaved a sigh of relief from behind
Heavens are full of mercies and kindness
I developed courage and grit that stayed
My determination, hard work and perseverance
After a while gave me success as it paid
I got greetings and good wishes incessant
From strangers and acquaintances all the same
The bouquets looked thorny and barbed
As I was reading the senders' names
Oh, please spare me! stay back where you are

I do not need to any association make
My success and my failures are both only my own
Please let me live in peace and do not hatred for you rake

53. Dreams

I dream of a life full of joy and bliss
An idyllic paradise where tranquility dwells
Harmonious peace and melodic symphony
Musical enchanting, like temple bells
I dream of a beautiful garden of blooms
Fragrance embraces every soul living
Motley petals, spectral hues and colors
Believe in goodness and righteous giving
I dream of freedom to all the women
Where she has her liberty and her say
Her passions are realized and wings not clipped
Her dreams beyond the horizon each day
I dream of a society free of evil biases
Races and colours and religions insignificant
Every heart throbs for love and camaraderie
And such prejudices become totally irrelevant
I dream of a space which is lively and cheerful
Where happy resonant echoes play
A day of complete utopia rules the air
May all my dreams be realized one day

54. Breaking barriers

She was taught the meaning of the scarlet color
And asked her to be wary if it's visible any day
She then had to stay back home in seclusion
And furtively tell to whoever she may
She rolled up her eyes in bewilderment
As her soul blazed in shocking rage
She was the modern girl of this century
An outspoken brave lass full of courage
She broke the myth and allegory of the past
And showed she could cope with and deal well
The woman has the strength infinite
and wouldn't be held in confinement in a shell
Her immense infinite potential today
Is like the blaze of the feminine wrath
She has travelled a long way to reach this point
A courageous road, a spirited path

55. Trembling unsureness of love

It had been many years into her wedlock
And she was not getting her bundle of joy
The family pursued the couple to visit a doctor
It was heartbreaking to know that
There wouldn't be stork visiting
Tears welled up which breached her eyes
Sorrow was wounding the heart and soul
She felt incomplete and more so
now unsure of her husband's love
He had become quiet and distanced himself
Indifference became his language
Though his lips did not say anything
His body language said it all
She was a barren woman who had ruined his life
He could have got a better what he deserved
Now a life was before him which would be colorless
And a liability in the form of a wife
She was insulted and harassed, tortured mentally
Her friends took her to another doctor
Who saw her reports and declared
Yes, 'tis true that there won't be a baby
But its because of the man who is at fault
The friend threw the report on the man's face
And showed him the mirror true

Now it was the turn of the man
To be unsure of the woman's love for him

The woman wiped her tears and held his hand
Taking him to an adoption center
Both now have a charming angel in their hands
and are sure of their love for her.

56. A silent dark night

A silent dark night
Dusky silhouettes of trees
Eerie silence chilling spine

Milky moonlight guides
Starry sky, a canopy
wavering flickers shows path

Uncertain heart chords
seeks guidance for aching souls
Follows divine starlit skies

57. The pillars of strength

You held my hands when I was young
Taught me to walk and held me from a fall
As I staggered to and fro and stumbled oft
You'd give me steady strength as I stood tall
You made sure I was full even while you'd stay hungry
You stayed awake the whole night
Nursing me with cold sponges and love
Making my days and future bright
You'd wake me up without fail in the morning
As grudgingly I opened my eyes in bed
You'd be busy readying everything for my school
When I'd just wish you attended school instead
You were my pillar of support in my tough days
You gave me an ear and a shoulder to cry
You uplifted my dying spirits and crushed morale
Raising my self-esteem to a newer high
Today your hands are wrinkled as they tremble
Old age has been getting the better of you
I'm here with you as a pillar of steel
Holding your hand, I shall never leave you.

58. My heart is speaking

I don't know how to be silent when my heart is speaking
When beautiful and motley blooms blossom
And its fragrance, the breeze carries in its bosom
I smile in gleeful cheer
When there is injustice inflicted on the weak
My heart melts while my soul speaks
and my essence drops a silent tear
When there is love brewing up and I know
My heart feels it yet refuses to show
I want to confess yet my lips quiver
When I want to drown in the ocean of desire
I can feel within the passion of fire
I undermine my emotions for fear
The heart knocks at the door of my essence
What's your significance and why's your presence?
Why not say what you feel within
Fueling sufferings, pain and agony in
I now have opened up my heart, my soul I bare
Every emotion, with passion and elan I share!

59. Chase your dreams

A beautiful journey called life
Bridled with ease, hardships or Strife
Difficult to tread sometimes on arduous trails
We tend to avoid difficult paths and crawl as snails
Hey ! get up and open your wings to fly
The sky is the limit and you are meant to soar high
Unleash your potential that lies latent within
Give it a tug, knuckle down and glide with a spin
Life gives you chances hidden and concealed
Make used of every opportunity: crack every deal
This beautiful life just comes to us one time
Follow you passions, dream to realize your goal prime
Every moment is a gift from above, live your life king-size
Live and let live with love as this is a blessing prized.

60. Unlearn, learn and relearn

The ocean of knowledge is unfathomable
A single life very short to everything learn
Each morning ushers in a new beginning
For us to focus, imbibe and knowledge churn
Everyday is new, as it puts a step ahead
Yesterday's learning becoming obsolete day by day
One has to unlearn first to remove the archaic bits
Gearing up to welcome new facts coming your way
Learning is extensive and has no limits
You may learn even from children small
Sometimes knowledge is imparted by the ordinary
Only that you should be prepared to take it all
Keep your mind open and house no prejudices
Let learning flow like a pure and clean tide
Be willing to learn newfangled ideas,
Take everyday learning in your stride !

61. My secret

A doctor has many secrets in his heart
As he is bound by a bond of trust
The patients share their woes and diseases
To keep them preserved is ethically a must
Sometimes one is faced by a dilemma of sorts
When it's a secret hidden by husband from a wife
The doctor cannot breach the unsigned faith
And cannot be the reason of a strife
There are occasions when a patient confides
How she had been in childhood raped that day
Or how she was molested by an elder family member
And how she has come a long way
Patients sometimes tell you their bedroom woes
Outrageous, which you cannot ever dare to spill
You keep that secret in you till you die
It may seem routine, though a task uphill

Secrecy and privacy are part of my profession
I hide and keep them in layers which never bare
They shall live and go with me to the grave
I am a trusted keeper of secrets-so I declare!

62. The truth dipped in ink

Poetry is not mere words
That rhymes in ornate tapestry
It's not a bejeweled piece of artifact
Which beautifies a façade in embroidery
Poem is a powerful tool that brings forth
Emotions dripped in righteousness
Values etched in ethics and principles
Every pen a powerful sword
The nations tangled in wars and destruction
Witness to anguish, poverty and deaths
Poetry watches helplessly as bombs and bullets pierce
Multitudes of innocent chests
Poetry sheds tears of sorrow over scattered corpses
Putting forth its opiniated views
Yet becomes feeble and powerless to cease
The monsters of destruction and tyranny
Poetry has the power to uncover lies
That is dripped in sugary honey
The ink spills, smudges and stains leaving a mark
Exposing the liars who throttled truthinhumanely

63. The red door

Everyday as I'd see the locked red door
I'd be curious to know and explore
Why is it locked and colored thus?
What's behind this locked door
I stopped and put my ears to the wall
Trying to hear if there's any clamor
I could hear clattering of metals
And subdued voices like a murmur
I thought of reporting it to the law
And to get to the bottom of the fact
The cops opened the door by force
And were shocked to see the horrible act
Minor girls were shackled and chained
To be trafficked for organs and flesh trade
There were cries of horror as the door opened
The young lasses were given emotional aid
The cops resolved to nab the perpetrators
The red door was now always open wide
The victims of cruel and beastly crime were saved
And now the red door has nothing to hide

64. Triversen

The vast blue sky
Was lit with stars
Twinkling bright
The moon peeped
From the sky
On a cold night
The clouds hovered
In black cloaks
Hiding the moon
Branches swayed
To the breeze
Laden with scent
A small drizzle
Poured on souls
To drench it
Divine nature
A beautiful view
That blesses all

The triversen is a loose form of sentence-long tercets developed by William Carlos Williams

Triversen rules:

Each stanza equals one sentence.

Each sentence/stanza breaks into 3 lines (each line is a separate phrase in the sentence).

There is a variable foot of 2-4 beats per line.

The poem as a whole should add up to 18 lines (or 6 stanzas).

65. Screams

The screams which were never heard
As I clung to the umbilical cord
Of my mother in her womb
I could hear treacherous tactics
To make her womb my tomb
The girl inside me trembled
And gave a scream startled
I want to live, I want to breathe,
But I was losing a lost battle
The kith and kin of my mom
Told her I was of worth none
As the girl child in the legacy
Could never be better than a son
The son carries the bastion forward
A girl is a liability on all
You feed her and she goes off to marry
While a son with you stands tall

I was pierced and poked with tools
My screams reached on deaf ears
I write this epitaph for myself
With the fallen blood mixed with tears

66. The bride

Bedecked and bejeweled
She dreams of the big day
Her family is living to see
Giving her off in marriage
She wants to study more
And spread her wings to soar
But the society cries foul
What if she goes astray?
Give her hand in marriage
Before she grows more
She says she has many dreams
To realize which she'd need support
The family urges that she as a couple
Would gain more than she alone
The day arrives when everyone's happy
And waits to see the "happily ever after' sight
One big work unloaded; a duty done
She's given off in marriage
The red saree gets shredded in threads
The jewels are taken away from her
Her books kept aside
Her wings clipped and torn
Her dreams wiped and she chided
She's now married woman
Who has no right to live as she wishes.

67. Isn't he dangerous?

He is there smiling with all children
Holding them in embraces and bosom
The pedophile hidden inside the beast
Isn't he dangerous?
The Godman who has enormous followers
Gives sermons and helps infertile woman conceive
Behind closed doors, inseminating the helpless women
Isn't he dangerous?
He requests you to carry his parcel
The parcel has incriminating stuff
Drugs and weapons concealed within
The innocent you is framed unawares
Isn't he dangerous?

68. Numbers

What a wonderful role these numbers play
Right from our birth and on every day
You are born on a particular date
Numerology then calls that number your fate
You remember every birthday by a number varied
That number becomes important to be stored and carried
Numbers and examinations are fond of each other
The more the numbers, the higher you're up the ladder
Then come the number game of your salary as money
The more digits to it, the more your worth in society
Number has a role in your family size
Lesser the number of progenies, the more you're wise
Numbers do not leave you while you age to grow older
Your behavior is then expected to be mellowed and milder
Oh numbers! You affect our lives every moment, every day
Dates, months, age and weight all numbers are at play!

69. Motherhood

That moment when every woman
Turns from a mere lady into a mother
Carrying her most precious gift in herself
A piece of herself she holds and nurtures
Enduring innumerable difficulties and maladies
She smiles and protects that prized possession
Who is going to lift her to the status of a mother
She drenches it with love and her own blood
Blossoming and fostering it to a replica of her own
She has chiseled it to a figurine of life with soul
Her warmth and shade keeping it alive and kicking
Till it separates from her as another entity
Whom she puts to her chest and breathes love
Her unconditional love makes her the baby's second soul
Her heart aches in her pain, rejoices in her smiles
The mother is connected emotionally
with the baby for her entire life

70. Arabic poetry-The stages of love

Al-Hawa (*The all-powerful eye: the gaze*)
The gaze! oh it's mesmerizing
A deep ocean with
unfathomable depth
Those brown magnetic eyes
Intensively pull me in attraction
As I lower my gaze in shock and coyness
I cannot look into
those valleys of charisma
Lest I should drown in the chasm
And get lost into the maze of his charm
Alaqah *(the attachment*)
Every morning is your
wandering presence around me
Clinging to my heart and soul
I see you here, there, everywhere
I see you even in your absence
And can feel your gazing mesmerizing eyes
As I jolt in an excited fervor
The nights are equally empty
And I can feel your shadowy silhouette
All around me, chasing me with those
Magnetic eyes….
Kalaf (*the infatuation*)

I cannot but wait to see you
and capture you in my eyes and heart
When you walk past me with that enticing smile
I feel your physical hold and hug over me
I can actually feel you tugging on my soul
Your absence makes me restless
My teary eyes look for you all around with
Multitude of emotions
If only we could be together
Always in bliss, of ethereal ecstasy
Embracing and entwining our souls forever

In Arabic, the word for love is Hubb, حب, Hubb has many degrees and the lover has many states, from affliction to madness. In Arabic, love has many degrees but I have written only about three.

71. The cat and his zing

The boss was getting tougher day by day
I had a good mind to put a stop to his ways
But who'd bell the cat? Reasoned out a friend
Tis not PAW-ssible to put this to an end
Then we all found out a PURR-fect solution
We Meow-nipulated him into a clever negotiation
If he now got catty, we'd all write mails
Splash it on the graffiti as catty-tails
The cath-letic boss missed his brisk walk that day
Curiosity was killing the cats that were coming his way
Our Claw-ver tactics made the mice play
His eyes poured like cats and dogs that whole day
We are happy as if the cat a canary swallowed at last
The boss is running around to sweeten the kitty fast

72. The dark love

Colors speckled, pretense galore
Love! you look innocent and pure
Deceit and deceptive demeanor
Hidden in layers of masked attitude

Trust broken and shattered to shreds
Will I'll be able to love again?
Exploiting emotions which are wiped out
Leaving me alone writhing in pain

73. Oh! woman thou shall be judged by all

Oh! woman thou shall be judged by all
Every stagger or stumble would be counted as a fall
You are the epitome of ethics and morality
You are no human- and that is your specialty
You shall be celebrated for days nine twice every year
Men would worship you, revere you or even bow with fear
You are the Goddess of wealth, knowledge and nerve
The deity of strength, devotion, fertility and Verve
Without you the world comes to a pause
The progeny and the future would all go for a toss
But then you will be the target of all distrust
Why did your eyes not look down when his was full of lust?
No it wasn't his fault as he is a man with a masculine virtue
It's You whose onus it is to behave divine, and true
The man will decide if you are unfaithful or chaste
If he has misunderstood you, your matrimony may not last
He has the authority to throw you out of his life
Just because the neighboring ogler stared at the wife
Oh woman! who are you? A mortal in this evil world
When even Sita endured the slander which on her was hurled.

74. Hurt me no more

The cool breeze and the mild drizzle
Hurt my soul as in the fire of reality they sizzle
My wounded heart finds no succor
Growing pain has lacerated it to the core
The pretense of your subtle mild care
Only makes my injured and battered essence bare
I do not like your caressing, cafuning mild
The storm within me is raising its head wild
I need some time to put myself in a shell
Cocooning me in a dark corner to dwell
No, I do not want your twinkle dear stars
They remind me of my happiness lost afar
Let me cry as tears in cascades pour
Oh macrocosm ! hurt me no more!

75. The sun and the moon

Beautiful milky celestial angel
I love your silvery translucent beam
Mild and cool, soothing and calm
How ethereal and magnificent is your sheen
Singing an aubade, for the beautiful day
Oh, golden orb! cheerful are your ways
Your sunshine drenches the world in light
Making the people happy and bright
Oh, beatific crescent soaked in luminescence
Gentleness and tranquility are your gifts in cadence
Hey Sol! the mornings sing and chime with your glow
In the presence of your divinity, every soul bows
Both the sun and the moon met in the horizon
Where one set and the other rose as a reflection

76. The temptations

In the castle of righteousness
Lived a beautiful princess of happiness
Her father King Joy kept her in high spirits
Giving her good values and virtues
The moatoutside the castle had a flow of goodwill and kindness
The drawbridge checked back the flow of anything insidious
At a distance, in the enchanted city of Greed-lust
a monstrous temptation as a dragon was scheming
To break open into the castle when all were sleeping
He took a boat of five senses into the waters
The Dragon was obstructed by the people
Thousands of men and women tried to stop the dragon
Who ultimately entered the castle
Capturing the princess of happiness
The whole castle was turned into one of sorrow
All happiness vanished and the castle was now
An arena of immorality and wrongful deeds
King Joy was brutally killed and thrown in the water
Now there is only gloom and despair that resides in the castle
The devil of temptations progressed as righteousness died.

77. The end is the beginning

Life is a circle with
arduous turns and bends
At every point there may be
the beginning or the end
A new journey begins when
one ends and is complete
The feeling of achievement
leaves one happy and replete
But life flows as a river
and carries in its drive
Innumerable wishes and dreams
which their destination arrive
A seed sprouts into a plant
which later its leaves sheds
Spring gives rise to winter
which later in summer ends
The cycle goes on and on
and there's no beginning or end
Every end is a new beginning,
So, let's this message send!

78. POCKET POEMS

This is a genre of poetic verse which is characterized by its extreme brevity. In other words, a pocket poem is a short poem.

Imayo- Success

Those passions that I pursue, the dreams that I chase
Lessons of perseverance ne'er ever give up
Don't rest till you get your goal, go the extra mile
The fruit of success is sweet, 'twas worth the efforts

Sedoka-Musical heavens

The singing blue sky
Stars on its lap twinkling bright
beyond reach yet within sight

on the ether high
wandering clouds croon floating
Creating a symphony

Lento-Your haunting memories

Oceans of sentiments when overwhelm

Emotions when turbulence create

Broken, my essence winced in agony

Unspoken words would pain mitigate

Raining thoughts of you, drenched me

Paining, my inner core cringed

Remaining pieces of my soul calmed

Sustaining on your memories, I hinged

Pensee-Beauty

Beauty
Is not skin deep
The pure heart and soul reflect
Angelic, pious, charm dazzles
eyes of the beholder

Breccbairdne

Do not go away
I shall need your sweater
No It's not yet over
Winter is no better

When there is sunshine
It'd be very easy
Your sweater I'll return
As it turns more breezy

Ida's sunshade

The golden ball is set ablaze
Its spewing fire wrapped in wild breeze and the wind-prickly,
itchy
Looking for shady trees, bare-footed I run and the earth
feels like burning charcoal beneath
Plenty of melon musk, water and lemonade, ice cream and shakes
that chill parched tongue and souls
Indoors, home now
Feel like heaven
Give sunshine not a tan

Flamenca-Forever yours

Drenched in the rain with you
Teary, dreary, soul beams
Blossoms of joy bloom
Creating memories
Etching every delight

Essence

Scarred sore soul cries in pain
Hurt injures core again

Whitney

Fragrant breeze
Flowing in ease
Tugs my soul
Waving leaves tease
Whiff of scent
Swaying the blooms
Enchanting gentle zephyr

Sijo

she waited for him all these years, with crying soul
and flowing tears
He went away ignoring her regretting soon for that blunder
He returned to find he had missed the boat while she found love again

Magic 9 poem-The magic of nature

Beautiful morn with sunshine brightening the day

The golden ball just rose up above the horizon

Dew drops shining leaves as in the breeze they sway

Fragrant whiffs of air that pervade the morning new

Silvery sheen on every bloom as the sun casts it rays

The azure sky with meandering balls of cotton
Perfumed petals of blossoms with a motley array

Chirpy feather friends now together twitter in unison
Giving us bountiful blessings in this ethereal way

Telestich-Flame

The maze of memories of you that engul**f**

Silent tears with cascade of sadness abysma**l**

Leaving me in a gush of dismal dilemm**a**

My love , you cannot ever fatho**m**

My parched soul drenches in your endearing drizzl**e**

Octet-Your love

Your emerald eyes where I'd drown

Embrace that fills the abyss

warm smile to cheer me up

An ocean of life

I cannot live

a moment

without

you

Limerick

The pack of wolves were on a hunt

They met a pig which couldnt grunt

The monkey saw this from the tree

And wanted some camaraderie

It jumped to hug and did a stunt

Epitaph

Here lies Johnny dumb as stone

Who took a fortune from me as loan

Reminders went on deaf ears

Reinforcing all my standing fears

From where do I get my dough now?

You rest, but I've a long way to go now!

Glossary

1.**Imayo** is a 4-line Japanese poem that has 12 syllables in each line. There is a planned caesura (or pause) between the first 7 syllables and the final 5.

2.**Sedoka** is an unrhymed poem made up of two three-line katauta with the following syllable counts: 5/7/7, 5/7/7. A Sedoka, pair of katauta as a single poem, may address the same subject from differing perspectives.

A katauta is an unrhymed three-line poem the following syllable counts: 5/7/7.

3. **Lento**, a poetic form created by Lencio Dominic Rodrigues, is named after it's creator.

A Lento consists of two quatrains with a fixed rhyme scheme of abcb, defe as the second and forth lines of each stanza must rhyme. There is no fixed syllable structure to the Lento, but keeping a good, flowing rhythm is recommended.

4. **Pensee** is a five-line, non rhyming patterned poem that is both fun and easy to create.

5. The B**reccbairdne** is an Irish quatrain form. Here are the basic guidelines:

Quatrain (or four-line stanza) form

Five syllables in the first line; six syllables in the other three lines

Each line ends with a two-syllable word

Lines two and four rhyme

All end words consonate

(Consonance is the act of repeating consonant sounds)

6.**Ida's sunshade** is a form of poetry that when centered, the poem looks like a parasol or an umbrella.

The number of syllables are represented by x. Take a look!

xxxxxxxx (8)

xxxxxxxxxxxxxxx (15)

xxxxxxxxxxxxxxxxxxxxxx (22)

xxxxxxxxxxxxxxxxxxxxxx (22)

xxxx (4)

xxxx (4)

xxxxxx (6)

7.The **Flamenca** is a Spanish quintain (or 5-line stanza) form with a staccato rhythm meant to replicate the click of heels by flamenco dancers. The flamenca goes by a few other names, including seguidilla gitana (or Gypsy seguidilla), playera, and/or sequiriya.

Here are basic guidelines of the flamenca:

- 5 lines
- lines 1, 2, 4, and 5 have 6 syllables
- line 3 has 5 syllables
- lines 2 and 5 assonate

8. **Essence** is a rhyming hexasyllabic couplet with internal rhyme with a twist. Normally in English prosody "internal rhyme" refers to a word within the line rhyming with the end word of that line or the end word of the previous line.

9. **Whitney** is a titled syllabic form, created by Betty Ann Whitney, has exactly seven lines.

Syllable Pattern: 3/4/3/4/3/4/7

10. **Sijo** is a Korean verse form related to haiku and tanka and comprised of three lines of 14-16 syllables each, for a total of 44-46 syllables. Each line contains a pause near the middle, similar to a caesura, though the break need not be metrical. The first half of the line contains six to nine syllables; the second half should contain no fewer than five. Originally intended as songs, sijo can treat romantic, metaphysical, or spiritual themes. Whatever the subject, the first line introduces an idea or story, the second supplies a "turn," and the third provides closure.

11.**The Magic 9 Poem** is a simple nine-line poem with a rhyme scheme of ABACADABA.

It has no other rules or regulations.

The rhyme scheme is deceptively easy to remember since it is literally just the word "Abracadabra" with the r's removed.

12. **Telestich** is a poem in which the consecutive final letters of the lines spell a name.

13. **Octet** is an invented form introduced by Dr. Laura Andersson. It is simply a diminishing octave.

The Octet is:

- an octastich, a poem in 8 lines.
- It is syllabic, 8-7-6-5-4-3-2-1 syllables per line.
- unrhymed

14. **Limerick** is a rhymed humorous or nonsense poem of five lines which originated in Limerick, Ireland. The Limerick has a set rhyme scheme of : a-a-b-b-a

15. **Epitaph** is a short poem remembering the life of someone who has died. Like elegies they are commemorative. Epitaphs are shorter than eleigies and are used on gravestones.

www.ingramcontent.com/pod-product-compliance
Lightning Source LLC
LaVergne TN
LVHW010609160826
845677LV00013B/3331

* 9 7 9 8 8 9 1 3 3 2 4 7 8 *